HANOK TODAY

HANOK
TODAY

NANI PARK and JONGKEUN LEE

 Hollym

Carlsbad, CA and Seoul

HANOK TODAY

Publisher   Sangbek Rhimm
Director   Songhee Lim
Editor   Minji Hahm
Designer   Hyehee Lee

Copy editor   Richard Harris

First published in 2023
by Hollym International Corp., Carlsbad, CA, USA
Phone 760 814 9880
http://www.hollym.com   **e-Mail** contact@hollym.com

 Hollym

Published simultaneously in Korea
by Hollym Corp., Publishers, Seoul, Korea
Phone +82 2 734 5087   **Fax** +82 2 730 5149
http://www.hollym.net   **e-Mail** hollym@hollym.co.kr

ISBN 978-1-56591-513-8
Library of Congress Control Number   2023938906

Printed in Korea

Hanok, traditional Korean houses made of wood-frame construction, have existed across the Korean Peninsula since the Joseon Dynasty and have been a staple of the Korean architectural landscape for centuries. Since they originated in the late fourteenth century, *hanok* houses and structures have been used primarily as residential spaces. Recently, however, it's become more common for them to be used as coffee shops, boutiques, restaurants, and event spaces. With *hanok* becoming trendier and more popular in recent times among younger generations and foreign visitors, I felt the need to create yet another book on *hanok* to showcase their other side: commercially used *hanok* spaces. Due to my diverse background in the arts, I have always been an aficionado of all forms of art. In recent years, I have grown to appreciate even more mediums of art, particularly architecture and design. My interest in *hanok* stems from my enthusiasm for architecture, history, and, presently, the multitude of uses for traditional Korean houses.

In my first book, *Hanok: The Korean House*, I showed the world what lies behind the walls of private *hanok* homes where people currently reside. Now that the public has become more aware of *hanok* living, I wanted to do another book on the subject, specifically one dedicated to different *hanok* that aren't only used as living quarters but also as creative spaces that serve as retail stores, offices, and even vacation rentals. The more *hanok* business operators I spoke with, the more I realized the significance in sharing the unique stories and experiences of the businesses operating in *hanok* and the owners' commitment and passion for the preservation of these historic homes.

Upon interviewing a number of people who ran these *hanok*-operated businesses, it quickly became apparent that these operations commonly performed better commercially precisely because they were in *hanok* structures. The neighborhood coffee shop isn't just a coffee shop—it's a *hanok* coffee shop. People come to the coffee shop not just for the coffee, but for the *hanok* structure itself. These coffee consumers enjoy being in a space that's different from anywhere else. Some are nostalgic for the traditional Korean houses they grew up in, while others are curious to indulge in something new they've never experienced before. The speakeasy bar, modern art gallery, and getaway rental all become more compelling because they inhabit one-of-a-kind *hanok*. These traditional Korean structures— even modernized ones—provide culturally unique and architecturally beautiful experiences that concrete buildings cannot offer.

Walking through the Jongno District of Seoul's northern Gangbuk area, one will find *hanok* structures in clusters or sporadically placed between skyscrapers in the busy business district. There are currently over 900 *hanok* homes and establishments located throughout the Gahoe-dong, Samcheong-dong, Wonseo-dong, Jae-dong, and Gye-dong neighborhoods, all of which are popular among tourists and Koreans alike. One well-known collection of *hanok* homes and mixed-use properties can be seen in Bukchon Hanok Village, which is situated north of Cheonggyecheon Stream in the Jongno District. The beauty of Bukchon lies in the sheer number of *hanok* that are found in the area, as *hanok* villages of its size are today very limited, especially in the heart of northern Seoul.

While Bukchon has become the most well-known *hanok* village in Seoul, its sleepier neighbor to the west of Gyeongbokgung Palace, Seochon, has been experiencing quite the renaissance in recent years because of all the trendy restaurants, bars, and businesses scattered around the *hanok* village. Most young Seoulites today will have heard of the up-and-coming restaurants and bars taking over the F&B scene in the quaint part of Jongno made up of both residential and commercial *hanok* that dot the west side of the palace.

Historically, *hanok* were designed to blend the elements of the outside with the inside—a harmonious flow of the surrounding environment incorporated into the home. However, in recent times, the upkeep of *hanok* structures has become increasingly challenging, as space can be limited, materials are hard to come by, and finding a qualified professional to maintain the original building is difficult. I started to wonder how these *hanok* business owners were able to sustain their operations in a *hanok* and yet still appeal to their customers. While many of the *hanok* buildings of Bukchon and its surrounding areas are newly constructed, it is still possible to see older, more traditional *hanok* homes that remain throughout the neighborhoods today. Although many of them have been able to keep their traditional facades and structures, it is sometimes difficult for newer *hanok* to maintain all the traditional characteristics or keep from adding modernized changes to ruin the integrity of *hanok*.

In the past, *hanok* were designed so that they would not disturb their surrounding environments. Thus, they were built as spaces that connected the past and the present. This is a concept we need to remember when building *hanok* in today's day and age in order to sustain the survival of *hanok* for the future. However, as a business owner is usually focused on providing services and, ultimately, the bottom line, a *hanok* business owner is also concerned with the preservation of the *hanok* structure as not only an add-on to the overall experience but also as an act of cultural responsibility.

I have carefully selected 15 *hanok*, both modern and old, residential and commercial, to show readers the diverse range of *hanok* that are operating businesses and providing residential spaces today, and to share the stories behind the business concepts, inspirations, and challenges of the proprietors. I invite you, my readers, to explore these *hanok* through these pages and photographs, and to visit these establishments to see the businesses firsthand.

Nani Park

"Pitter-patter…" Raindrops fall on my camera. I move all my equipment under the eaves and wait for the rain to ease up. I listen to the sound of it falling as I watch it drip off the eaves. It's been raining quite a lot during the *hanok* photo shoots for this book. If there's rain in the forecast, the photo shoot is usually postponed. This time, however, we proceeded with taking pictures even though the weather wasn't so good. To reassure the worried author, Nani Park, I said, "We're going to see a mixture of both clear and cloudy conditions with each passing day, right?" Even as I said those words, I was capturing the changing expressions of *hanok* at different moments, some with the rain and wind. This is because I wanted to fully embrace this feeling of enjoying nature while simultaneously adapting to it. When I'm in a *hanok*, the soft light seeps through paper pasted over the wooden window frames, and the distant scenery feels closer. The sculptural quality of the rooms that look like they're overlapping each other comes across as a continuous grid of angles, but it actually makes the viewer's mind feel more relaxed. In this book, I've done my best to capture these small sensations one feels inside a *hanok* in each frame.

In an age when things are so rapidly becoming digitalized, *hanok* convey the values that have been continuously sustained for centuries. The concept of small, simply designed rooms that expand in size by opening up the *deureoyeolgae* doors upwards and bringing nature into the house through borrowed landscapes is still present in modern *hanok*. This is expressed in various forms, such as minimalism which pursues moderation and simplicity, free transformation according to necessity, and naturalness. Through this project, I was able to see how well restaurants, accommodations, and workrooms—places commonly seen around us every day—come into harmony with *hanok*.

The Swiss Hanok is a modernized Korean house that embodies both contemporary architecture and the concept and meaning behind traditional *hanok*. It's not simply a Korean-style house with an old chest added; rather, it's an architectural structure that sought to encapsulate the concept and spirit of *hanok*, something that has been passed down from long ago, starting with the design phase. The idea of not opposing nature—something that can be felt in the way the house is arranged and the structure of the rooms—as well as the freedom that does not constrain creativity represent the very spirit we so desperately need today. At the same time, these concepts epitomize the value and heritage of *hanok*.

Jocheonmasil, which embraces modernization; Häbre Seoul, which combines a Swedish aesthetic with *hanok*; Danmul, which provides a small yet infinite workspace; and Hanok Essay Seochon, which serves as a peaceful retreat in the city center, are all unique and beautiful contemporary *hanok* expressing the individuality of each house. Each one of them is, in essence, living *hanok*. Like traditional Korean clothing (*hanbok*), they warmly embrace us, allow us to rest comfortably, and fully express our individual style. In this regard, *hanok* is like clothing that protects our bodies! It's my sincere hope that through this book I can share and empathize with the emotions felt by people who live and work in *hanok*, most notably beyond understanding merely the architectural or interior design aspects.

I'd like to express my gratitude to Nani Park, who worked alongside me for a considerable amount of time, the owners of each space who shared their beautiful *hanok*, and the staff who participated in all of the shoots. I'll put a wrap on this photo shoot with the dream of sharing a *hanok* studio of my own with readers one day in the future.

Jongkeun Lee, Photographer

CONTENTS

HÄBRE SEOUL

This *hanok* is particularly special to me, as it is the first of hopefully many projects to come that I have personally worked on with my family. We have lived in *hanok* before, but this was the very first collaborative project where each of my family members added some amount of input for the design, concept, and ideas. As the author of numerous *hanok* books, it only felt fitting to debut this newly built *hanok* in my latest edition.

Nestled in the unassuming side alleys of Seoul's increasingly popular Seochon neighborhood, there lies a carefully disguised Scandinavian getaway right in the heart of this sleepy *hanok* village. The byproduct of a multicultural family of both Swedish and Korean descent, this passion-fueled project was born from our family's desire to share both cultures with foreign and Korean guests as the ultimate homage to traditional Korean architecture.

Häbre Seoul was conceived from the idea of bringing our summer home in northern Sweden, where we spent many memorable summers in the past, to Korea so that we could share our experiences with family and friends without leaving the country. Häbre originally meant "storehouse" in Swedish, but has now transitioned to loosely mean "guest house" or "country house." For our *hanok*, it represents a blend of Korean architecture with a Swedish design flair. Häbre Seoul is our way of showing our love and appreciation of Scandinavian design. As a multicultural family, we understand how special our situation is. We have been given the unique opportunity to learn the particularities and characteristics of more than one culture, which we are excited to return to our community in Seoul.

We wanted to find a way to offer our guests a Swedish getaway without leaving the city limits of Seoul and experience the tranquility of *hanok*, something that is a rarity for most Seoulites. Without altering too much of a traditional Korean *hanok* design, we wanted to highlight the original features of the *hanok* structure while also showing how the traditional homes can be brought into the modern age, specifically with our bold and colorful wallpaper and contemporary kitchen style.

Rebuilding the *hanok* into what Häbre Seoul is today and turning it into a short-term homestay business, we have learned that it requires the combination of talented architects and designers with prime locations and attentive owners. Understanding the background and concept of Häbre, we decided to work with architecture and design firm Z-Lab and Stayfolio, a luxury online booking platform for curated stays, to bring Häbre Seoul to life. Our partners brought life back into the framework of the structure through the invaluable input of our family to create the perfect ambiance of a Swedish-Korean *hanok*.

Covered in "Paradiset" wallpaper by
Josef Frank for Svenskt Tenn, the floor-
to-ceiling vision of warmth, color,
and maximalist design was hung to
complement the minimalist furnishings
of the *hanok*.

Häbre Seoul provides visitors with a unique and tranquil hideaway in the busy city of Seoul, somewhere guests can unwind as they submerge themselves in a freestanding half bathtub and relax.

Dual views of the courtyard from the dining room. The bold industrial look of the red bricks enhances the mix of traditional and modern elements of the *hanok*.

ABOVE A collection of carefully selected Scandinavian furnishings and antique pieces placed throughout the *hanok* to complete the overall Häbre look.

OPPOSITE Cook a favorite meal in a simplistic, uncluttered but fully functioning kitchen.

DANMUL

first met Jangwon Son in a Japanese cooking class, where we instantly bonded over our love of cooking and food. We got to talking about the new *hanok* he was building in honor of his love of food—he was creating an entire *hanok* kitchen. I was immediately intrigued because I'd never heard of an entire *hanok* being dedicated to someone's passion, but Jangwon Son was building a "test kitchen" or "laboratory" for all types of traditional and non-traditional food and drinks, both Korean and non-Korean.

He has been carefully curating the space and filling it with items he's been collecting for years from his travels and studies, and has finally completed Danmul, which means "sweet water." He explained why he chose to build his kitchen laboratory in a *hanok*, telling me, "Since I've lived abroad for more than half of my life, I wanted to return to my home country to express my unique identity in the form of a *hanok*, and incorporate all the various cultures I've experienced so I could see my footsteps through sight and sense, not just words or writings." He continued to describe a *hanok* as "warm as a grandmother's embrace, where people have non-stop conversations and are surrounded by the beauty of the structure."

As a former fashion and industrial designer, Jangwon Son not only has a background in the design world, which you can clearly see in Danmul today, but has also developed his experiences in food and beverage by learning about everything that goes into the human body and why it is so important to share that mindset with others. When designing Danmul, he wanted to incorporate the feelings of a variety of textures, using stainless steel for his kitchen, which is surrounded by the wood-frame *hanok*. By pairing together contrasting textures and materials, he wanted to create the ultimate sensory experience when entering and enjoying the *hanok*.

When I asked him about his *hanok* and the concept of his business, he mentioned the time he spent in Europe and how he wanted his return to Korea to reflect the experiences he had when living abroad. His *hanok* and his business are tangible extensions of his footsteps, explaining, "While traveling in Europe, I remembered the small concerts and theater stages that were held in alleys and squares. As I built my small *hanok*, I thought of the inside of the *hanok* as a stage and designed the *hanok* where the courtyard became the seats for an audience to watch. Here you can enjoy being in the moment and impart upon the audience a bright energy for the future."

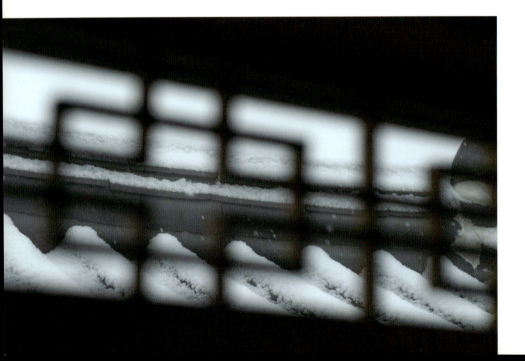

LEFT Dangling above the sleek gray wooden table are mini chandeliers from the personal collection of the owner acquired from his travels all over the world, particularly the United States and Europe, and complementing the Nordic dining table chairs, which are also from the owner's collection.

FOLLOWING SPREAD The kitchen distinctly stands out with its manufactured Italian stainless steel Alpes-Inox appliances in an all-wooden natural environment of a wooden *hanok*, bringing together the stark contrast of manmade and natural materials in perfect harmony.

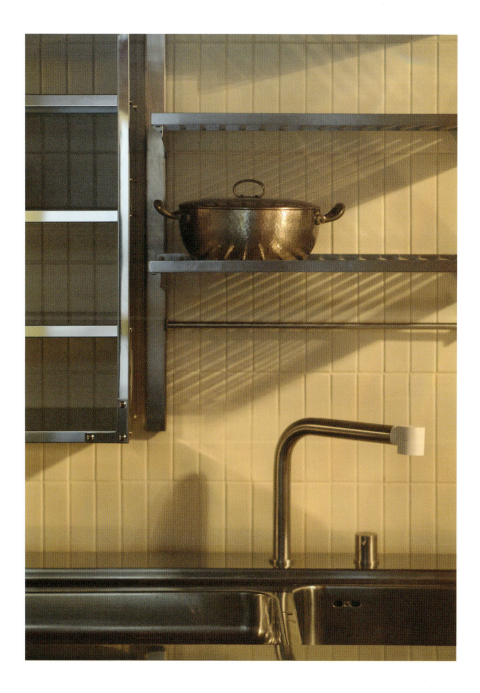

ABOVE The simplicity of solid concrete accented with paintings by contemporary artist Ko Jiyoung complements the *hanok*.

OPPOSITE French wall consoles hold handmade ceramic pieces made by various artists and the owner.

A collection of earthenware sits atop a
bookcase from French luxury furniture maker
Moissonnier, all of which comes from the
personal collection of the owner.

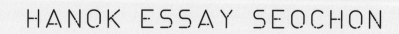

HANOK ESSAY SEOCHON

With an intimate atmosphere, customized attention to detail, and design-savvy accommodations, Hanok Essay Seochon goes beyond a mere boutique B&B experience. Tucked along a small, quaint alleyway of Seochon, the vacation rental, or "*hanok* stay," is surrounded by a maze of other *hanok* structures and is a conceptual fit to the architectural legacy of this historic neighborhood. Hanok Essay Seochon is a participating *hanok* on Stayfolio, an online accommodation platform featuring mainly unique, high-end, quality places to stay in Korea, with Hanok Essay Seochon being one of their more popular *hanok* stays.

While carrying out research for this book, I came across this popular and celebrated *hanok* stay on social media, and I knew at once that I had to see it for myself. Upon meeting Seokwon Jeong, the owner of Hanok Essay Seochon, I discovered that he had a copy of my first book, *Hanok: The Korean House*, and that he had used my book as a visual inspiration for his *hanok*. I was humbled and flattered that my book could inspire his design concept for his business and that I could see its successful operation in person.

By definition, a boutique hotel puts great emphasis on design and style. Hanok Essay Seochon transcends the elements of a boutique stay through its style, elegance, and foundation of the owner's vision: relaxation and serenity in the middle of a chaotically busy city. As Jeong sees it, "Unlike apartments in the city, there is a unique feeling of relaxation to a *hanok*, where a small yard with trees and grass connects to the indoor space, and you can hear birds, the sound of the wind, and the sound of footsteps in the neighborhood alley."

When I asked him why he chose the name "Hanok Essay," he answered, "An essay means writing freely without any special rules. Hanok Essay Seochon is about *hanok*, but it is freely reinterpreted in a form that is convenient and familiar to modern people. The visible space has all the features of a *hanok*, such as Korean traditional fences, roof tiles, and roof structures with rafters, but the everyday parts are familiar and comfortable, such as the chairs, sofas, beds, and even a bathtub in the middle of the home. Instead of traditional Korean paper windows, a large glass window was used so that you can see the small yard with a traditional Korean wall from anywhere indoors, and feel the flow of time and the season, including sunlight, moonlight, wind, snow, and rain."

Seoul's Urban Redevelopment Project started in the early 1980s to redevelop dilapidated neighborhoods, deteriorated homes, and inadequate infrastructure, which expedited urban redevelopment efforts, building and maximizing the allowable space for newer, more modern concrete buildings but losing traditional neighborhoods along the way. The current refocus of the project is to boost the local economy by emphasizing and conserving the characteristics of the original neighborhood. Seochon is one of these historic neighborhoods, and Hanok Essay Seochon embodies the new urban redevelopment project by renovating traditional structures and strengthening the social economy. Jeong backs this up by saying, "I believe that not only is working with *hanok* a great business opportunity but it's also a chance to contribute to the community through efforts to preserve *hanok* at the same time. *Hanok* properties can be properly utilized to suit the tastes of modern people."

FOLLOWING SPREAD   Hanok Essay Seochon embodies the true meaning of alfresco, or "in the open air." This *hanok* harmoniously combines rustic and contemporary elements in a tranquil and serene environment. Refurbished wood rafter beams and unfastened doors blend the outdoors with the indoors, specifically the bathtub in the center of the *hanok* that was constructed with an original wood covering.

With floor-to-ceiling windows, Hanok Essay Seochon allows sunlight to permeate the house and for visitors to experience the changes in light throughout the day.

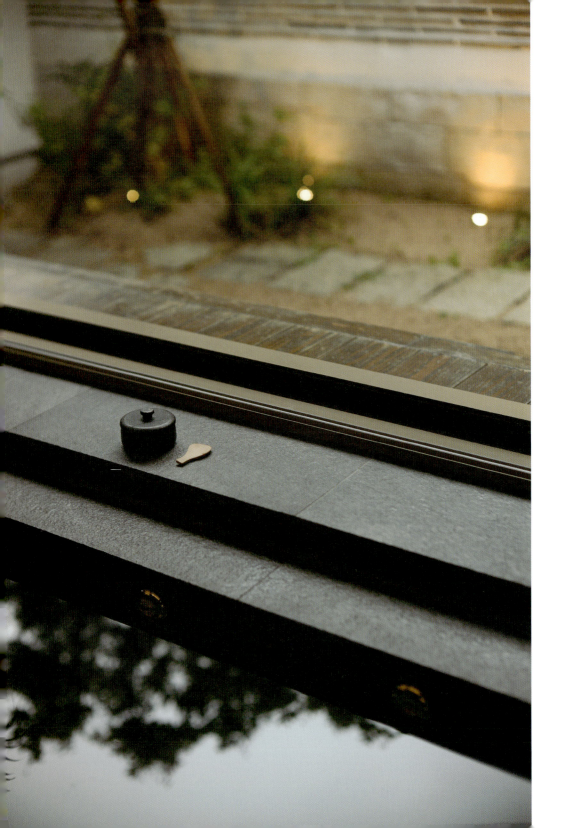

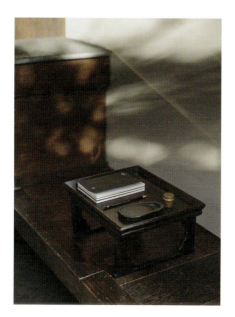

ABOVE   The owner added small traditional Korean touches throughout the *hanok*, like the tea set and guest book table for foreign guests, in particular, to experience.

FOLLOWING SPREAD   The lounge was built with the idea of guests enjoying relaxing downtime with coffee and music while sitting by a warm, cozy fire.

BAR CHAM

Serving innovative and creative cocktails infused with and inspired by traditional Korean liquors, Byungjin Lim, the owner of Bar Cham, has been making its mark on the Seoul cocktail scene since it first opened in 2018. I happened to stumble upon Bar Cham a few years ago when the front door was left slightly ajar one day and curiosity got the better of me.

Taking a peek inside, I was shocked to see a long wooden oak bar with fully stocked shelves of both Western and Eastern liquor bottles behind it. While he did not specifically seek out a *hanok* to open his business, he has successfully built Bar Cham into the popular cocktail bar it is today in precisely this kind of intimate space, highlighting the ambiance of traditional *hanok*.

Lim said his interest wasn't in the architecture itself, but rather the environment surrounding the business. "It was an 'injured' *hanok* made up of old and fragile trees, nothing particularly special, but seeing the way the enclosing trees in the ceiling intersected with each other, I saw the potential of the space," Lim explains.

OPPOSITE   The masterful specialty of Bar Cham is its original, authentic Korean-inspired cocktails.

The renovated bar consisted of removing old reinforcing bars and refurbishing the structure of the H-beams while conserving the traditional design principles of *hanok* to embrace and accept its natural habitat, not challenge it. Instead of going against the grain of the wood and cutting in straight lines, he used the natural curvatures to enhance the design and structure of the building. Much like his mixology concepts, he sought to embrace the natural essences of the *hanok* just as he does with liquor and complement the individual tastes instead of masking and challenging the flavor of the drink. "I wanted to build a space where my guests could enjoy the bar environment as much as they enjoy the cocktails, which is why I made such an effort in renovating the *hanok* to what it is today," Lim says with pride.

He now sees his business as a cultural responsibility to create a legacy for future generations and is committed to promoting Korean culture to both Koreans and foreign visitors of all ages through his unique concoctions. Operating a business in a *hanok* has been challenging for Lim, mostly because of the care and maintenance of the space, which needs to be handled with a delicate touch. He wanted to create an inviting and comfortable space that was welcoming and inviting from the outside to the inside, explaining, "I think *hanok* structures are one of Korea's most intuitive elements that visually show our culture. By virtue of the fact that you are in a *hanok* structure, Bar Cham is able to showcase Korean culture through not just its Korean-based cocktails, but through the surrounding structure itself as well. Even if I were to open Bar Cham in Gangnam or New York City, without the surrounding features of a *hanok*, the bar wouldn't be the same and it would lose both its visual and cultural value. Wouldn't it be better if there were more *hanok* being utilized as commercial spaces? If I can help create memories in this space, then I must take careful responsibility for Bar Cham's role in promoting and preserving Korean culture."

FOLLOWING SPREAD   A quaint little bar tucked in an unassuming alley way of Seochon, which completely lives up to the definition of cozy: "assured ease, warmth, shelter, and friendliness."

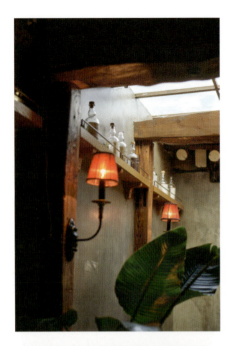

Full external view of Bar Cham, where on any given evening, customers line up for hours to enjoy their unique cocktails.

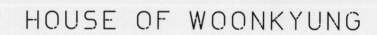

HOUSE OF WOONKYUNG

At over 400 years old, Woonkyung Gotaek, or House of Woonkyung, has been a significant landmark in Korea for centuries and a great contribution to preserving Korean history. House of Woonkyung has been managed by the Woonkyung Foundation, a non-profit public interest foundation, not only to preserve the *hanok* house but also to promote cultural programs and raise awareness for the foundation's efforts. They say timing is everything in life, and we were extremely fortunate to have our scheduled photoshoot at the same time as the exhibition *You Are My House*[*] by the artist Jeonghwa Choi.

Given the significance of this particular *hanok* and its extensive preservation efforts, I wanted to include the late politician Lee Chai Hyung's historic home to memorialize the house that has contributed so much to protecting Korean traditions and culture.

[*] This was a limited engagement exhibition in 2022. Normally, House of Woonkyung is not open to the public.

OPPOSITE   Silk Road, 2020

As you enter the house, you are first greeted by two mannequins dressed as police officers. This work, titled *Funny Game* (1998), was created by designer and artist Jeonghwa Choi.

"*Hanok* is a living building. It's a building that changes according to the weather and humidity, so it lives and breathes with the changes of the seasons. At House of Woonkyung, we host a variety of art exhibitions and we have been surprised by the infinite amount of possibilities the *hanok* space provides with each installation," says Mee Hae Lee, Director of the Woonkyung Foundation and a descendant of Lee Chai Hyung, former Speaker of the National Assembly.

When asked how this *hanok* came to be, she described the background of the foundation, saying, "Located at the foot of Inwangsan Mountain, House of Woonkyung is where Lee Chai Hyung lived for 39 years, and for the next 30 years, the *hanok* was operated by the foundation and his descendants. It's a space that has been well maintained and managed, and it's existed for over 70 years based on one individual's life."

"The opening of House of Woonkyung to the public means more than just showing the well-preserved structure," Mee Hae Lee went on. "The time and historical significance of space, the life of the person who lived here—all of these things are protected and carried on here. I wanted to create an opportunity to share people's experiences with as many people as possible."

Lee highlighted the true meaning of *hanok* and the opportunities they present, explaining, "From a long-term perspective, *hanok* is our tradition and it must be kept as it is. It means a lot to us to find reasons to continue to coexist in the future through the inevitable changes to come. *Hanok* are truly unique and the possibilities they provide are endless—and the conversation about them is only just beginning."

Sehando (Winter Scene), 2018

ABOVE Me without You, You without Me Holobiont, 2021

FOLLOWING SPREAD (LEFT) My Beautiful 21st Century, Plastic Spring, 2022 (RIGHT) Bodhidharma and Venus, 2019

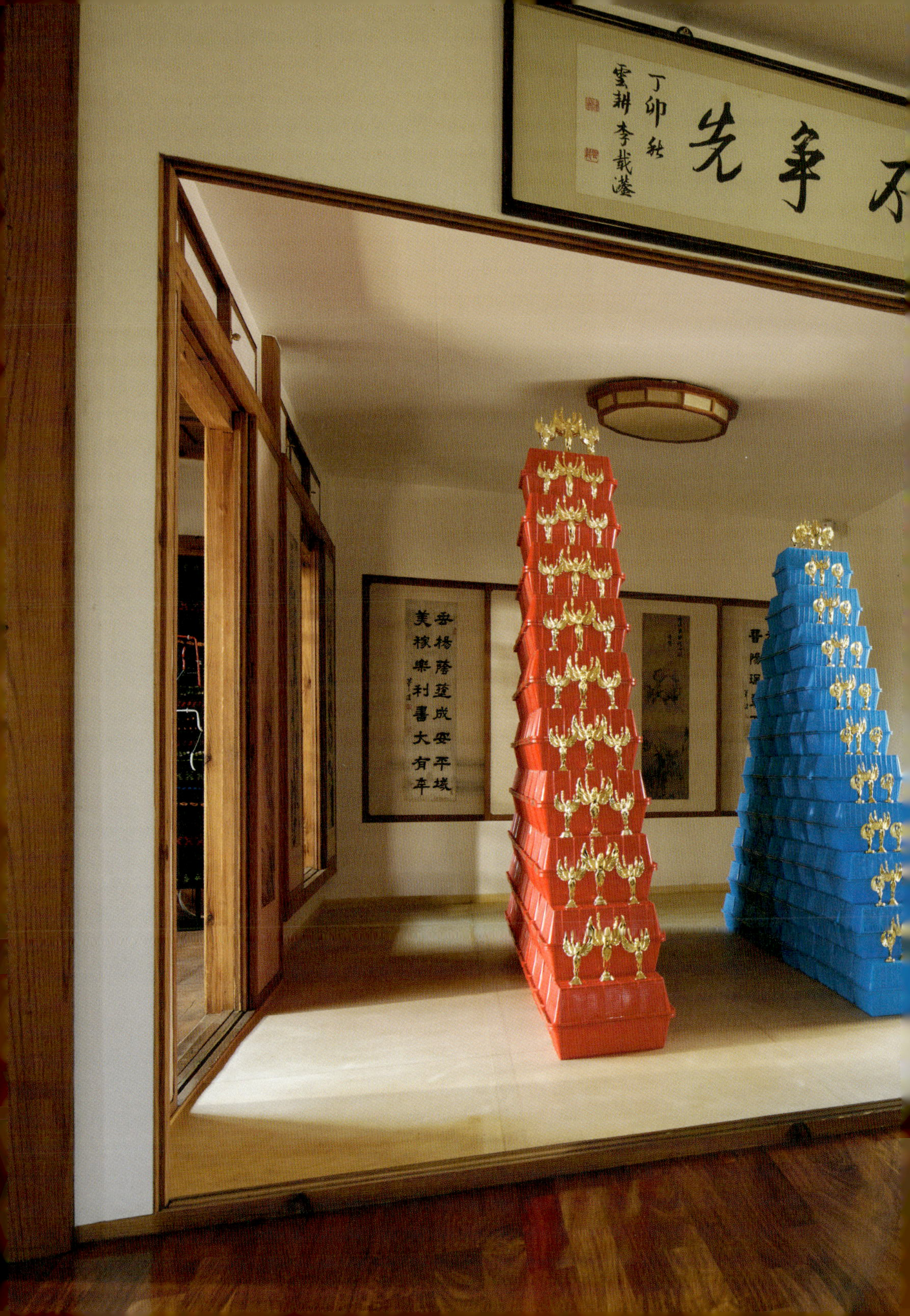

不爭先
丁卯秋
雲耕 李載瀅

ABOVE   Infinity, 2020

PREVIOUS SPREAD   Ajumma Numen, 2018

TOP   Beach Observatory, 2020
ABOVE   Love, Love, 2020

99

ABOVE Blooming Matrix, Bronze Pagoda, 2018

SWISS HANOK

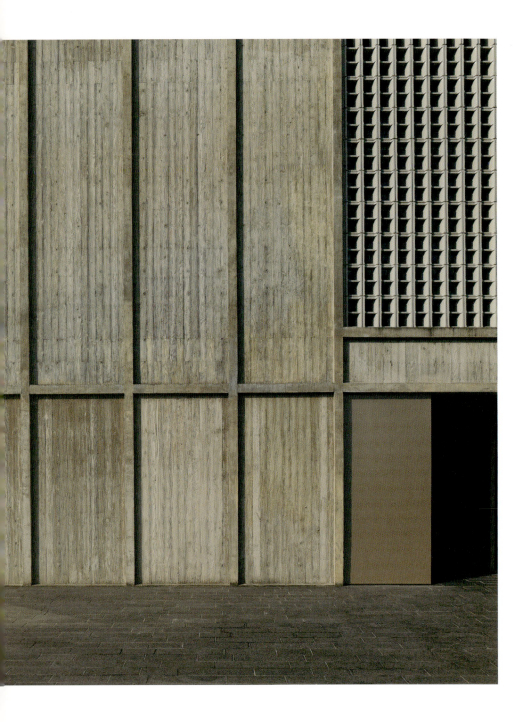

I was first introduced to the Swiss embassy in Seoul through the previous Swiss ambassador when they were in the process of building the current Swiss "Hanok" that sits behind Seoul's Gyeonghuigung Palace. At first glance, I wouldn't have considered the structure to be a *hanok* in the traditional sense of the word, as it lacked the feel, the essence, and the original architecture. But upon my continued visits to the embassy, and after speaking with the various architects that have worked on this project, I now understand their interpretation and have grown to understand what a contemporary *hanok* is today. As the finishing touches were completed on the embassy, I've found that my knowledge and vision of what a *hanok* embodies has also evolved, to the point where there is no right or wrong way to interpret art. Instead, I've realized that the origins and essence of *hanok* play a large role in what a contemporary *hanok* is in our modern society.

As Dagmar Schmidt Tartagli, Ambassador of Switzerland to the Republic of Korea, puts it, "The unique architecture was the result of an open architectural competition where 73 architectural studios from around the world submitted designs for the new Swiss embassy building.

PREVIOUS SPREAD   Located in the middle of the courtyard at the embassy, *Water Connection* is an installation art piece by Lena Maria Thuring. It consists of three hand-molded chains connected to the roof's eaves and gutters. When it rains, water falls down along the chain and passes through three stones that come from three different rivers in Switzerland: the Rhône, the Rhine, and the Ticino. The journey of the rainwater flows to the floor carving, and is reminiscent of the Han River in Korea.

The winning submission was from Burckhardt + Partner SA of Lausanne, Switzerland, with the code name 'Swiss Hanok,' and planned to embody a contemporary interpretation of the traditional Korean house with attention to Swiss architectural practices." She later adds, "The jury gave the following decisive reason: 'As much by its volume, a unitary and emblematic figure, as by its exterior spaces, which offer an identity, a representative and contextual courtyard, the project proposes a strong identity for the future Swiss embassy in Seoul. By preserving the memory of the place, affirming its exceptional character, and honoring its low and domestic volumetric drawing from Korean vernacular history, it asserts its singularity, that of an institutional program in the middle of a district with a future vertical silhouette.'"

The chief architect at Burckhardt, Nicolas Vaucher, explained why Swiss Hanok—and whether any traditional Korean house—was suitable to host the Swiss embassy in an interview with Marc Frochaux, editor-in-chief of *Tracés* magazine,[*] saying, "There are still traditional houses in the area, which we took the time to observe. All the rooms are arranged around a courtyard that serves as an exterior distribution and an extension of the house, with the facade here being mainly open. On the opposite side, the facade works as an enclosure protecting the dwelling,

[*] Marc Frochaux: Échanges constructifs: l'ambassade suisse à Séoul; entretien avec Nicolas Vaucher, Burckhardt+Partner, Lausanne, in: Schweizer Botschaften / Ambassades suisses / Ambasciate svizzer, Sonderheft TEC21, TRACÉS, archi, pp. 32–41

Deep and long eaves extend out from the roof to bring a sense of breathability to the building, with the materials used being all natural and carefully selected to reflect its surroundings and protect the house from the elements in all four seasons.

with fewer openings. Now, this organization corresponds rather well to the double constraint of an embassy: to protect and to assemble at the same time. Thus, it allows for a qualitative workspace that is open to the courtyard, yet remains sheltered from the exterior by a perimeter facade wall, which is made of concrete. The courtyard at the centre can therefore be used as a meeting place, as well as a representative space."

"We are very satisfied with the architecture of the embassy, as it beautifully combines both Korean and Swiss architecture. It is an attractive and functional platform to promote dialogue, to bring people together, and to develop political, economic, cultural, and scientific relations between our two countries. Recently, the Swiss Hanok hosted a symposium on contemporary *hanok* architecture with the Seoul Metropolitan Government. Korean architecture has also been a hot topic from the Swiss side. For example, Swiss and Korean universities have launched an academic exchange program called ARC-HEST to study the working environment in each country in conjunction with the local culture and architecture. The strong

traditions, use of advanced technologies, and direction towards a sustainable society—traits that both Switzerland and South Korea share—have paved the way for this international cooperation," says Ambassador Dagmar Schmidt Tartagli.

Not only is the Swiss Hanok a testament to the blending of both Korean and Swiss architecture styles and cultures, but it also shows Switzerland's commitment to achieving net carbon neutrality by 2050. The Swiss Hanok implemented ecological green technologies in order to reduce its carbon footprint through the installation of solar panels for electricity, geothermal energy for heating and cooling, and a water harvesting system for cleaning and gardening.

The external facade of the Swiss embassy serves as a bridge between the cultures of the two countries, and every piece of commissioned artwork and installation reflects the joining of two countries, intertwining the collaborative mediums.

Traditional Korean lattice design is seen throughout
the Swiss Hanok with its linear wooden slats across the
window frames, along with stunning paper works by
Swiss-based design studio Atelier Oi, a trio of designers
renowned for their architecture and design work.

The captivating interplay of light and shadow highlight the glazed ceramic grid, showcasing individual ceramics and the display as a whole.

Interior furnishings designed by the Swiss-based design team Atelier Oi.

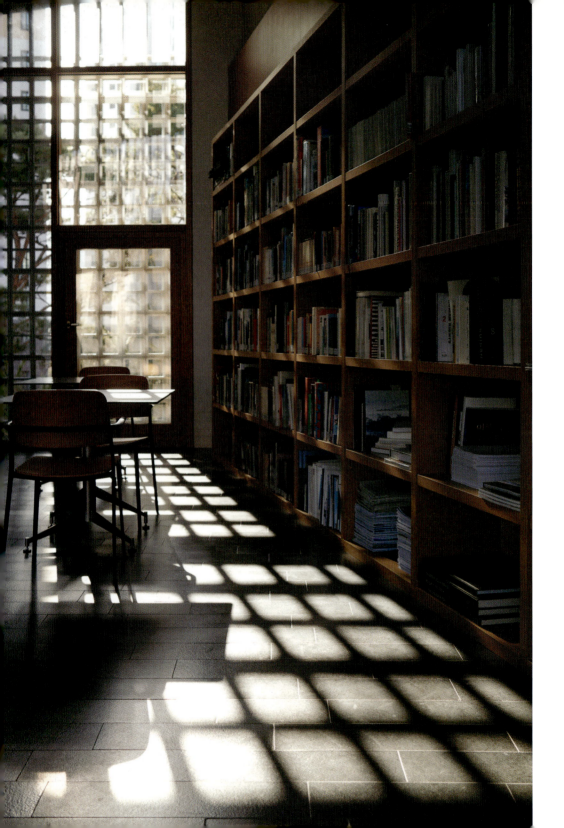

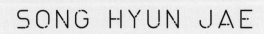

SONG HYUN JAE

誦絃齋

A stone's throw away from Gyeongbokgung Palace in Jongno, Kukje Gallery has been leading the way in the Korean art scene for the last few decades in modern and contemporary art, while also promoting Korean history and traditions with the Kukje Gallery Hanok, Song Hyun Jae, and other exhibitions. When I first learned that Kukje Gallery was building a *hanok* behind their world-renowned gallery, I knew it would be something special. Not only did they fill the *hanok* with beautiful art pieces and books to educate its visitors on Korea and art, but they also invited artists and leaders from around the world to show them the true beauty of *hanok*.

When asked whether *hanok* was an act of cultural responsibility, a contribution to Korean society, or a unique business opportunity, Boyoung Song, Managing Director of Kukje Gallery, responded by saying, "It's definitely a combination of all three. As our world is continuously developing on all fronts (i.e. technology, globalization, culture), I sensed a noticeable urge to harken back to the traditions and legacies that created the foundations of who/what we are and have formed our society today. Song Hyun Jae shows how we can live within tradition, but at the same time fortify the traditional *hanok* with contemporary interventions that enhance its relevance in our times."

The interior of the bookstore encapsulates a sense of calm and tranquility. Natural wooden bookshelves and wood tables with clean, simple lines are a common theme throughout the store.

She went on to explain, "In terms of the level of interest coming from overseas, Korea is enjoying its heyday. To all visitors from abroad, the *hanok* is the best way to show our cultural heritage, local context, and the direction we're changing towards. Kukje Gallery, in terms of both its history and programming, has always maintained strong roots with our homeland. In the same spirit as our gallery's mission to consistently promote Korean artists and culture abroad, *hanok* seemed like the most appropriate and sensible next step."

The bookshelves are filled with rare and beautiful art books from the Kukje Gallery collection.

Hanok have been experiencing a bit of a renaissance in recent times with the increase in popularity of them across Seoul and the rest of the peninsula. "Even before the renewed recognition of *hanok* these days, the cultural legacy of this uniquely Korean architecture has always been preserved in the form of museums and *hanok* villages around the city, namely nearby Bukchon Hanok Village. In whichever shape or form, the tradition of *hanok* has always stayed with us throughout the centuries, but it is a newfound idea that *hanok* have been incorporated into business models. As with *hanok* residences that are still with us today from the 14th century, I believe that *hanok* offices, shops, and other spaces for work and business will remain as a longstanding staple," says Song. With respect to Song Hyun Jae, she adds, "In renovating the age-old architecture of the original *hanok*, we paid particular attention to the outdoor courtyard, or *madang* in Korean. We conceived the courtyard as a unified space with the interior, unifying the floor with different shades of granite. Hence, once you open the lattice windows and sliding doors, all the spaces merge together."

OPPOSITE The courtyard features a stone bench by American neo-conceptual artist Jenny Holzer.

RIGHT Wooden art works by Emile Kirsch, a multidisciplinary artist based in France.

BELOW Broom collection by Danh Vo, a contemporary artist.

A cozy tea room adorned with furniture from Teo Yang Studio's Eastern Edition line.

Given Boyoung Song's background in the art world, it's interesting to hear her opinions on *hanok* in relation to art and architecture, in addition to the lifestyle it provides. As she explains, "*Hanok* is different from prevailing [mainly Western] canons of architecture, such as Gothic, Rococo, Neoclassical, and such. *Hanok* not only refers to the architectural style, but also a principle and way of living. In a way, *hanok* is more holistic and in this sense very contemporary, as each home/building is built in full consideration of its surrounding environment. For example, in the northern regions of Korea, which tend to experience colder winters, *hanok* tend to have a rectangular shape with a central courtyard, as seen with Song Hyun Jae, whereas *hanok* in the southern regions are built as a more open structure."

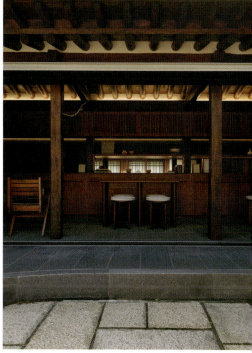

Boyoung Song goes on to add, "Song Hyun Jae is not only a place to read and study, but also to experience art in a uniquely Korean context. Any work of art can change completely when shifted to a new context/setting, and Song Hyun Jae sheds new light onto works by artists whose works were shown at our already existing gallery spaces. A Lucio Fontana, which is currently installed in my office, changes completely when it's moved from a crisp white cube space onto the walls of a *hanok*—it creates a dialogue that transcends continents and disparate centuries."

The *Mesmerizing Mesh* exhibition by South Korean artist Haegue Yang.

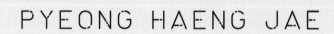

PYEONG HAENG JAE

W hen I first met Mark Tetto, an American businessman from New Jersey, he was
living in a modern apartment complex like the majority of the population in
Korea. As a newly arrived foreigner moving to Seoul, I suggested to my Korea-curious
friend that he should try to live in a *hanok* if he wanted to truly understand Korea and
what it is to be Korean. Some Koreans of certain generations have unique memories
of either living in a *hanok* or visiting relatives who lived in a *hanok*. Although the
familial connection of *hanok* living is a rarity for younger generations, some have
explored the *hanok* living experience through visiting *hanok* coffee shops, restaurants,
hanok stays or Korean heritage sites, such as palaces or museums. Although Mark
Tetto's home doesn't operate as a business, I wanted to share his unique perspective
of a non-Korean living in a traditional *hanok* and share his personal experience of
living in a Korean home, which led him to believe in the importance of preserving,
promoting, and conserving the historical value of *hanok*.

Since moving into a *hanok* home, Mark Tetto's experience in Korea has
completely changed. Describing his move from an apartment building to the
traditional Korean home as "an important step to deeply experience and learn about

Korean culture," he has since incorporated himself into the Korean entertainment scene and has become a spokesperson for Korean artifacts. With his unique *hanok* experience, he has had the opportunity to share through social media, essays, photos, newspaper columns, and public lectures the one-of-a-kind beauty, appeal, and historical significance of *hanok*, and has ultimately introduced more people to this beauty and why it needs to be preserved and protected.

"I have seen living in a *hanok* as being an act of cultural responsibility and a contribution to Korean and global society. I thought it would be a unique opportunity for me to personally learn more about Korean traditional culture, and hopefully an opportunity to share that culture with others. As a foreigner, I thought I had much to learn from this traditional style of home with which I had not been familiar, and I also thought I might be uniquely able to share this experience with other foreign friends by inviting guests to my house or by sharing my photos and thoughts about *hanok* through social media," says Mark Tetto about his continued *hanok* experience.

Western-influenced bedrooms filled with Asian artwork, most notably: photo of a moon jar by Koo Bohnchang, *Someone's Window* photo by Heewon Kim, and a ceramic lamp designed by Teo Yang.

ABOVE In traditional times, *hanok* houses had kitchens that were located in a separate building outside of the main house in order to reduce the risk of fires. Today, they are suited to fit contemporary and fully equipped kitchens with an open concept dining area like this one.

PREVIOUS SPREAD With its warm wood tones, the *daechung maru* provides a distinctive and peaceful space that fuses the old and the new. In the center is a customized coffee table personally designed by Mark Tetto, and which was inspired by *hanok* doors.

It's been a pleasure to see Tetto's journey of growth and transformation in Korea since first relocating to Seoul to moving into a *hanok* and now becoming a positive proponent of Korean culture and lifestyle. In his own words: "*Hanok* is more than just Korea's unique and culturally significant style of traditional architecture—it is much deeper than that. It is a philosophy, a way of living. It is a space that can transform and elevate one's thoughts, which can cultivate one's interests and heal a person."

153

OPPOSITE   The metal hook, or *deulshoe*, is not only ornate but is also functional and holds the folded latticed exterior doors up so that the warmth of the sun can permeate throughout the house.

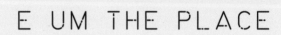

When asked to describe her *hanok* and the concept of her business, Kyungsook Mo, the owner of E Um The Place, compares *hanok* to a mother—strong and reliable, always preparing and adapting to the four seasons, beautifully simplistic once all her makeup is off, and bringing her heart into a home.

I was first introduced to E Um The Place when I was invited to a lovely art event there, and I distinctly remember being in awe of the structure of the *hanok*. I was struck by the courtyard garden in the middle of the building, the unobstructed view of Gyeongbokgung Palace, and the layout of the *hanok*, all of which helped make it feel more majestic compared to its actual size. Beautifully and simply designed, the inclusion of nature flowing from the outside inward makes it a desirable location for hosting events, art openings, and weddings.

OPPOSITE   The guardians of E Um The Place greet visitors as they enter the grounds of the *hanok*. *Haetae* are mythological lion-like unicorn creatures made of stone that protect one from fire.

OPPOSITE   Traditional partition screens and doors that are both conventional
and aesthetically pleasing.

As Kyungsook Mo describes it, "It's all about the harmony between nature and humans living in buildings. The house, built of wood, stone, and earth, retains its form with the presence of human breath and sincerity. It's the heart of a family that makes a *hanok* a home." Kyungsook Mo once considered making this her primary residence but decided it was best to share this home with the public and make it available to others in order to promote Korean arts and local artists. Rather than promoting the business, she hoped to bring a deeper appreciation to the cultural significance of *hanok* for generations to enjoy.

When initially renovating E Um The Place, the owner insisted on keeping the *hanok* as traditional as possible, but unfortunately the original *ondol* floor in the *hanok* had to be replaced due to environmental concerns related to the furnace fumes harming the surrounding trees. Maintenance is the primary challenge for all owners of *hanok*, as there are many factors to consider, including airflow, noise, environmental pollutants and, of course, the cost of materials.

When renovating this *hanok*, the owner recalled the many details that were taken into consideration, such as the types of soil, stones and trees, the interior and exterior landscaping, the seasons, climate and temperature, and so much more. The slightest changes to airflow or angles can affect the building acoustics, with even the opening and closing of doors altering the overall temperature of the *hanok*. Merging contemporary design while still embracing traditionally styled architecture was the unique spirit of this restoration, and blending the two styles was not an easy feat. The final product and overall ambiance of the *hanok* reflect the surrounding scenery, in which the owner, as she put it, "tried to create a space that connects the past, the present, and the future by communicating and collaborating with people from many different fields to strive for a *hanok* to withstand future generations to come."

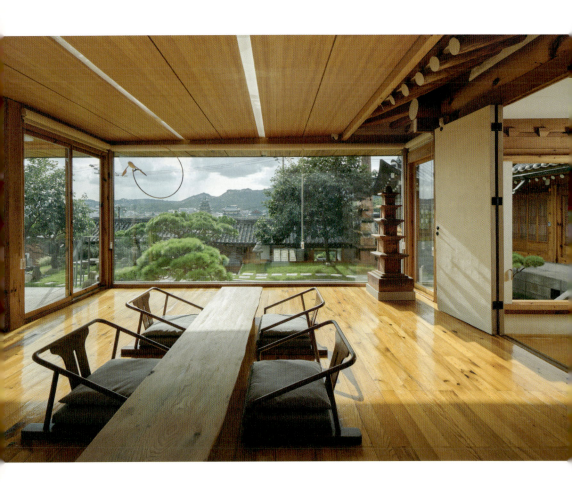

TEO YANG STUDIO

174

This is the third time I have decided to feature Teo Yang's *hanok* in my publications, and it still remains one of my favorite *hanok* in Seoul. Teo has transformed his *hanok* from a residential home to an office space and showroom in the most incredible yet natural way. Teo Yang, a renowned interior designer and the founder of Teo Yang Studio, has successfully changed the interior look of his home and workspace without altering the outer structure. I have chosen to include his *hanok* once again, as he continues to modify the interior look of his home with new and innovative styles to cater to his current projects and needs.

When I asked Teo Yang how *hanok* became such an integral part of both his personal and professional lives, he said, "I fell in love

with the beauty of *hanok* and I wanted to use and enjoy the space, regardless of its purpose. My goal was to share with more people the emotions and feelings of peace when entering this *hanok* space. In doing so, I have discovered that the theme of my studio is to focus on the contemporary expressions of local Korean culture and tradition, which was born from the *hanok* environment."

Since opening his studio in his *hanok*, Teo Yang's brand has continued to evolve around the traditions of Korea. He went on to say, "Living in a *hanok* itself gives an individual a brand element, and individuals soon feel the duties and responsibilities from the privilege of the *hanok* lifestyle. Through this, one finds that studying, researching, and promoting the rooted philosophies and beauty inherent in *hanok* are just another joy of living in a *hanok* home."

OPPOSITE   This Jean-Michel Othoniel glass sculpture adorns the *hanok* beautifully.

When walking into his *hanok* home and showroom, I'm always amazed at how he is able to harmoniously blend the beautiful historic elements of a Korean-style home with new and different Western features—and all the while maintaining the traditional flow of a *hanok* home. In blending different cultural aesthetics, Yang is able to stick with his studio theme through the idea that, as he says, "the element of Korean traditions, the modern Western touches—I believe the balance of both can show the past and the future within the amazing spatial elements of *hanok*."

"While *hanok* have a long legacy and history in our country, that doesn't mean they have to stay in the past," Yang goes on. "*Hanok* are always changing and progressing. I still find inspiration from my daily *hanok* life and I hope that *hanok* will become even more familiar in contemporary spaces today."

He concluded by adding, "At Teo Yang Studio, our various projects attempt to capture Korean beauty and philosophy gained through the *hanok* lifestyle for both domestic and foreign clients alike. By working in our traditional *hanok* setting, we are able to create future spaces using long-cultivated Korean touches."

PREVIOUS SPREAD   Within the personal living space of the *hanok* hangs an art piece by contemporary charcoal artist Lee Bae.

Teo Yang has a multipurpose basement that he uses for meetings and presentations, and which also doubles as a private home movie theater, unconventional for a *hanok*.

Set apart from his living area, Teo Yang's studio showcases products from his multiple affiliate companies, including furniture and perfumes from Eastern Edition, EATH Library, and Sinang.

MISHMASH

ABOVE Side view of *ilgak daemun*, the corner gate.

LEFT Archival wall that has been well preserved and remains intact.

Located along the outer western wall of Changdeokgung Palace, the contemporary Korean restaurant MISHMASH is a newly opened fusion dining outlet savoring nostalgia while creating unique experiences for all of the senses. A beautifully constructed two-story *hanok* with picturesque views of Changdeokgung Palace, the culinary menu reflects its surroundings—the historical Summer Palace lies in the middle of a bustling concrete jungle of modern buildings, mixing traditional Korean cuisine with international flair.

I was first introduced to Chef Minzi Kim Wind, the owner of MISHMASH and daughter of a well-known restaurateur, through mutual friends. While her mother is now retired, gastronomy has always run in her family and she has continued to carry on the family F&B torch. Previously operating her restaurant in Itaewon, Chef Minzi Kim Wind sought out MISHMASH's home in its current idyllic location so that her menu could be heightened by the *hanok* environment.

Born and raised in a *hanok*, her mother was eager to build a *hanok* for commercial use and to create a space for her daughter to continue on her culinary

journey. Throughout her professional career, Chef Minzi Kim Wind garnered opportunities all over the world, but Korea has always been her foundation. She wanted to share her experiences and the *hanok* her family built with locals and foreigners alike. As she sees it, "Cultural responsibility, social contribution, and business opportunity—these were the prime reasons I wanted to operate my restaurant in a *hanok* and to share with the world my personal *hanok* relationship."

From the outset, there were a multitude of factors to consider when building this *hanok*, but that main reason had to do with modernizing historical architecture to reflect 21st-century times. Her mother wanted the structure to be visually inspiring, while also incorporating the conveniences of modern appliances, and to build a functioning space for MISHMASH with an uninhibited open and exposed flow.

While *hanok* are generally limited to one floor, in order to take advantage of the views of the neighboring palace grounds, they decided a two-story *hanok* was essential. The traditional *ondol* (underfloor heating) and separate kitchen and bathrooms of a typical *hanok* were also streamlined to allow the open space and modern amenities, such as air conditioners and air circulation systems, to seamlessly blend into the *hanok* design.

Cost was another factor to consider when building, as wooden materials made in Korea are neither plentiful nor easily accessible. Traditional wood for *hanok* must be aged, but forestation in Korea makes acquiring specific materials challenging, which is where importing materials becomes necessary. There were also governmental standards, regulations, and approvals to abide by for building a *hanok*. From planning to final design submissions, all designs needed to be approved by the related government agencies. Although the whole process—from inception to completion—was at times an arduous task, the end result of people admiring and complimenting the beams and rafters of the *hanok* make the process worthwhile and an experience recommended by the owner herself.

"If there are existing *hanok* or land sites that can be built in the future, I think it should be encouraged for social, cultural, and commercial purposes. The *hanok* lifestyle is not a temporary trend, and *hanok* structures symbolize Korean identity. They instill uniqueness and pride for future generations of Koreans," says Minzi Kim Wind.

ABOVE Ground floor coffee shop, unlatched and uncluttered, which is an essential component when incorporating the surrounding landscape.

OPPOSITE Original table designed by the owner, with stones from the city of Mungyeong, which translates into "hearing good news."

Blue and white tableware from Royal Copenhagen is used at MISHMASH.

ALMOST HOME STAY
HADONG

actually discovered Almost Home Stay Hadong, a *hanok* located in Hadong, which can be found in the southeast of the country, when I was visiting Gochang, in the southwest of the peninsula, a few years ago. When in Gochang, I was introduced to Kolon's lifestyle brand, Epigram, which has been selecting lesser-known cities to introduce the region's foods, traditions, historic sites, and cultures to the rest of the country and beyond. At the time, Gochang was one of the cities selected by Epigram to promote its unique characteristics, and later Epigram moved on to Hadong, where the Almost Home Stay *hanok* is situated.

Today, Epigram is attempting to revitalize the local economies of lesser-known towns and cities by collaborating with local small business owners and artists to bring new consumers to these areas. Almost Home Stay Hadong is one of the hallmarks of Epigram's Hadong project, where the eight-unit *hanok* stay represents Hadong's traditional culture by preserving the home's historical value in a modern, elegant design setting.

OPPOSITE   The east-facing room allows a billowing warm breeze to inundate the *daechung maru,* an elevated wooden floor connected to the main house.

Kyungae Han, Director of Epigram's Almost Home project, says, "Epigram ran a pop-up space called 'Almost Home' in Wonseo-dong in 2015, next to Changdeokgung Palace, so guests could have a special experience looking at the king's garden. Our brand's characteristics, such as using materials that match the surrounding nature coupled with a minimalist design, are highlighted in our traditional Korean-style stay structures."

She goes on to explain, "I wanted to provide an opportunity for modern Koreans who live in housing apartments, and have perhaps started to feel frustrated with apartment restrictions, with a new experience to actually feel and live the traditional *hanok* lifestyle with natural light and open spaces."

She adds, "We wanted to create a *hanok* stay that represented and co-existed with the local Hadong environment. We made efforts to convey these points and create positive synergies in the establishment of Almost Home Stay Hadong, which has since won an award from DFA Design for Asia. We were thrilled to receive the recognition from the award, but we were more excited by the memories we have created for visitors and the opportunities for the surrounding town of Hadong. Additionally, we wanted to create local employment opportunities to actually help the region, on top of promoting the region to non-locals."

When asked what the priorities of the *hanok* were, Kyungae Han replied, "Looking at the scenery from the *hanok*'s window, you can see the wide fields of Agyang-myeon and the Seomjingang River. I was looking at the picturesque scene and wondered what kind of people lived in Hadong. I wanted to know what experiences we can provide to highlight the region and what else we can do to help the city of Hadong."

She concludes by saying, "A person's mindset changes depending on their surrounding environment. A *hanok* is somewhere time passes slowly. The contents that fill a *hanok* should be chosen according to the characteristics of the specific *hanok*. The Almost Home Stay Hadong *hanok* was designed so guests can relax and feel rejuvenated. *Hanok* emphasize openness, rather than closure, and we want to encourage more people to travel to lesser-known places like Hadong to have new experiences in new regions, especially in traditional Korean-style houses."

A Western-style dining room in a *hanok* can be a unique fusion of traditional Korean architecture and modern Western interior design.

A folding screen *baekjaho* crafted by the Mono Collection is placed in the tea room to bring the space together nicely.

HOUSE OF CHOI

EYST 1779
YOSUKGUNG 1779

Settled along a river bank near Woljeonggyo Bridge, House of Choi of the 1779 Group consists of two types of *hanok*: a traditional *hanok* that houses a fine dining Korean restaurant called Yosukgung 1779, and a modern brick *hanok* that has been transformed into a cafe called Eyst 1779 by the current generation of the Choi family.

Gyeongju, Korea's ancient capital during the Silla Dynasty, is a city filled with national treasures and traditional *hanok* spread throughout the city. I first learned about House of Choi when I saw it was featured in a well-known magazine and then connected with them through the aforementioned *hanok* dweller Mark Tetto, who had met them on a recent weekend trip down to Gyeongju. Upon hearing about the beauty and creativity of this *hanok*, I knew I had to see it for myself in person. As it turns out, I was beyond impressed by not only the structures of the *hanok* themselves but also by the extensive efforts the family has made to preserve their family legacy and Korean traditions.

PREVIOUS SPREAD   EYST 1779 is not a traditional *hanok*. The impressive floor-to-wall red bricks form the introduction of this conspicuous building, which tempts passersby to explore this hidden historical gem with a modern design.

As Haeok Kim, CEO of House of Choi, told me, "I think the emotional experience and the discovery of beauty that we feel through our *hanok* are valid cultural values and assets we must preserve for the next generation. There is also a sense of responsibility as a member of the family, one in which we don't want to replace the traditions of the houses and families that have been inherited from generation to generation, but instead preserve the spatial beauty of our *hanok* with such history and heritage. I think of the House of Choi as a kind of public property and we want to provide the opportunity for as many people as possible to feel and experience the beauty and traditional beauty of *hanok*.

With a focus on food and beverage, House of Choi—on top of its well-respected fine dining restaurant and coffee shop—also makes its own line of traditional Korean liquor. Haeok Kim explains: "The legacy of tradition in *hanok*, Korean alcohol, and food has been handed down since ancient times, and has gone through a lot of people's hands. Today's era is moving faster, with mechanized and automated systems doing the bulk of actual people's work, but we must pause to make the necessary efforts to support, preserve, and pass on traditions. This is why we are making separate efforts through 1779 to deliver our traditional heritage to the next generation."

When asked what *hanok* means to her, Haeok Kim beautifully describes her views on how *hanok* impact more than just current visitors, saying, "A *hanok* is a space where the individuality and presence of its owner and surrounding region are overtly expressed throughout the structure, despite the framework and rules of what makes a *hanok* a *hanok*. It may seem uniform at times, but even the older houses that are over a hundred years old clearly reveal their own regional features, climate, and individual preferences of their owner. For this reason, if you take a closer look at any *hanok*, you will find that there are many stories inherent in its walls. The whole history of individuals, families, and neighborhoods permeates the space, and this serves as a kind of communication medium that connects one generation to the next generation. I hope the next generation will continue to add to this bridge we are building for them now."

The cafe houses cursive streamscape structures by prominent artist Chulan Kwak that are both aesthetically stunning and functional. They also serve as benches for patrons.

OPPOSITE Light illuminates a side building to showcase a four-story stone pagoda next door.

While unassuming from the outside, the stunning entrance to Yosukgung 1779 is grand, transporting visitors to a bygone era as they walk through the property. People are greeted at this magical place by trees all hundreds of years old. Visitors are also free to take a seat and peacefully sip on a cup of tea.

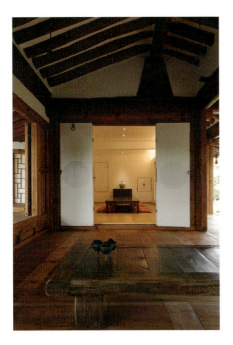

The House of Choi still uses traditional Korean recipes passed down in the family from generation to generation, all of which are shared with guests who travel from far and wide to have this fine dining Korean cuisine experience.

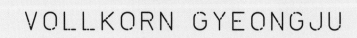

L ocated in the southern city of Gyeongju, Vollkorn Bakery has been attracting visitors from all across the peninsula to marvel at the beautiful *hanok* that has been converted into a German-style bakery. Formerly an oriental medicine hospital with an area of 3,000 *pyeong*, architect Jewon Han of Design Group SALK has transformed the traditional structure, which is now home to a modern cafe and bakery.

"When designing, I emphasize the harmony between the location of the building and its surrounding environment. My design philosophy is to include as much of the scenery as possible into the building so that it ultimately becomes a part of the structure. With this renewal project, I wanted to create a place for everyone so that more people could experience the beauty of *hanok*. I also wanted to maximize and preserve the structure of the existing *hanok*, such as its rafters and beams, rather than demolish it completely and rebuild it in a new style," explained Han when describing his initial thought process on the project.

PREVIOUS SPREAD   Once an acupuncture hospital, Vollkorn has been transformed into a popular cafe today on a sprawling property made up of multiple *hanok* buildings. The idiomatic expression of putting a smile on one's face is the motif of the "smiley face" theme of the cafe. The owners wanted this theme of happy people to permeate throughout the cafe as visitors enjoy their time here.

Innovative and whimsical, these herb medicine holders
have now been repurposed as bread holders.

Having designed and worked on a wide variety of building types, Han's sentiments towards the Vollkorn *hanok* project has been particularly unique and heartfelt. He went on to say, "One might say that *hanok* are uncomfortable and old, but I think well-preserved *hanok* are the best places to aesthetically capture the four seasons of Korea. As our ways of life change over time, I see it as the architect's task to solve the inconveniences of old-fashioned *hanok* life by combining modern functions with traditional *hanok* beauty."

Han also added, "In the case of this space, we wanted visitors to feel the special aura of the original space, so we were cautious when introducing any new materials and facilities that might harm the existing *hanok* in order to preserve its essence in today's environment. I think that the architectural style of *hanok* will gain greater recognition both in architecture and design here in Korea and abroad. Today's generation is increasingly consuming content and looking at our traditional culture in a new way, where *hanok* is once again in the spotlight for both commercial and residential spaces. I expect that more modern *hanok* will be loved in the long run as they become more popular in the content we consume and in relevant locations."

The traditions and historic significance of Gyeongju are prevalent in its landmarks, artifacts, and especially in its *hanok* structures, which are abundant throughout the old city. Han reflected on his experience of developing one of its older structures and what it means for Korean design, today and tomorrow, when he commented, "The experience of developing a *hanok* in Gyeongju was extremely valuable and I believe it is important to interpret and inherit the language of traditional Korean *hanok* architecture in modern architecture as much as possible. The most important thing is to keep thinking about what Korean design truly is and to study and implement how it can be incorporated into modern architecture. Through Vollkorn, we have learned more about its details and design language, so we will now try to apply these elements to future *hanok* projects we become involved in."

Wanting to restore this *hanok* to its original state while mostly modifying the interior space of the *hanok*, the owners highlighted the unconventional white ceilings and injected the whole place with contemporary touches reflective of the cafe.

OPPOSITE   Long corridors are a distinctive feature of Korean palace architecture. These corridors, known as *hoerang* in Korean, were designed to connect different buildings within the palace complex, providing a covered walkway for the king, queen, and other members of the royal family to move between buildings.

JOCHEONMASIL

While most of the *hanok* I chose for this project are concentrated in the Seoul area, I also wanted to include a *hanok* from the always up-and-coming Jeju Island. I especially wanted to showcase some of the island *hanok* that highlight the differences between a Jeju *hanok* and other *hanok* structures around the Korean Peninsula. This particular *hanok*, Jocheonmasil, was recommended to me by Z-Lab, the design firm working alongside Stayfolio, and is a highly sought-after *hanok* stay on Jeju Island.

Designed by Z-Lab, one of the main focuses of Jocheonmasil was to provide the experience of a *hanok* in its original architectural structure. The courtyard in the middle is surrounded by three separate *hanok* structures, which have all been renovated to reflect current amenities. The bathroom has been converted to a Zen spa, complete with a working furnace and cypress bathtub. The *hanok* is its own total environment, somewhere its uniqueness lies primarily in two traits: inclusive and exclusive. It's seamlessly intertwined with the neighborhood and blends in with other *hanok* and

PREVIOUS SPREAD A full view of the Jocheonmasil property, with three separate *hanok* houses. There is a wide range of styles of *hanok* where the structural autonomy differs from various regions, such as the large slate roofs to withstand the island's heavy winds or separated living quarters surrounding the main *madang* (garden) in the center of the *hanok* property.

homes on an unassuming street. And yet the open courtyard makes it feel exclusive and private, appealing to all seasons: shade and coolness in the summer, flowers in bloom in the spring, and a particular calmness and silence in the autumn and winter.

"Certainly the increased interest in *hanok* has expanded the concept of *hanok*, rather than solely the restoration of tradition. Z-Lab designed Jocheonmasil to capture a lifestyle that is both sustainable and sophisticated for future generations to appreciate," says Kyungrok Noh, one of Z-Lab's co-founders.

There is a wide range of styles of *hanok* in which the structural autonomy differs by region, such as the large thatched roofs to withstand the island's heavy winds or separated living quarters surrounding the main *madang* (garden) in the center of the *hanok* property. The island also has *hanok* with stone structures rather than traditional wood structures encased by stone walls to reflect the coastal environment. Although *hanok* styles may vary considerably from one owner to another, there is a cultural foundation that is shared, with each individual *hanok* able to be appreciated as a work of art, stylistically unique, and richly significant for the landscape of Korea.

Kyungrok Noh goes on to add, "Through Jocheonmasil, I wanted to preserve the time from when the *hanok* was first built and transport the stone house to our current day and age. *Hanok* isn't a passing trend. It's a deeply rooted and established asset and inheritance for people today. We should salvage and preserve all types of existing *hanok* throughout the widespread regions of Korea."

Authentic built-in cabinets original to the *hanok*.

Constructed *hanok* completely dedicated to be used as a hinoki wooden bathhouse.

OPPOSITE   Locally sourced volcanic rocks and heavy slate rooftops native to Jeju's original design were meant to withstand the island's strong winds and heavy rainfall.

277